Growing Up in Chicago

D. A. SLONE

authorHOUSE®

AuthorHouse™
1663 Liberty Drive
Bloomington, IN 47403
www.authorhouse.com
Phone: 1 (800) 839-8640

Published by AuthorHouse 10/20/2015

ISBN: 978-1-5049-5670-3 (sc)
ISBN: 978-1-5049-5671-0 (e)

Library of Congress Control Number: 2015917069

Print information available on the last page.

Printed in the United States of America on acid-free paper.

Contents

In memory of my father, James Latham.

Prologue

At the age of five, my grandmother use to tell me that I was a precocious child. I did not know what the word meant at that time, but I knew that it could not have meant something bad because she would have a pleasant look on her face whenever she said it.

I always enjoyed learning and I attributed this mostly to my grandmother because she was at home with me after school and each day, she would go over my homework and work with me on subjects such as reading and math.

My adolescent years were pretty much like any other kid. My grandmother had already moved into her own apartment, so she was not there to help me with my homework after school. When I was eleven years old, I had to have surgery and I was out of school for approximately one month.

After graduating from high school, I attended a junior college for a short period of time before I decided to find myself a job and move out of my parent's house.

I usually found a job as a Secretary or Word Processing Operator. The pay was not great, but I was able to pay my rent and take care of myself.

After I started working at JDT's Magazine Distribution Company, I discovered how different some people can be when you are making a decent salary. During the time that I worked there, I felt as if I was in a constant battle to keep my job. There were numerous occasions when someone at my place of employment made false accusations and I received a suspension or termination letter from my employer.

I always responded truthfully when these incidents occurred, but in the end, it did not matter.

In 2012, I had an Arbitration Hearing after being terminated from my job in 2011. I just knew that the Arbitrator (an attorney), would not go along with the woman who made some false allegations. Unfortunately, I was mistaken and I did not get my job back nor did I receive any back pay.

During the time that I was working at JDT's Magazine Distribution Company, I was also involved in a couple of car accidents. I was not at fault in either accident. I was injured in both accidents, but I did not receive any compensation for my injury, pain and suffering. This was very disheartening.

I decided to write this book because I feel that I was treated unfairly at the age of eleven and throughout my adult life. I wanted to share my experiences with other people because I believe that there are far too many people in this country who have experienced the same type of frustrations and disappointments on the job and in their personal lives.

Chapter 1

Apartment on Fifty-Third Street

In 1965 I was sitting in front of the television in the living room. My family and I lived in a three-and-a-half-room apartment on the South Side of Chicago. At that time, black people could not find housing south of Sixty-Third Street because white people did not want to sell their homes to black people. This was one way whites practiced housing segregation in Chicago.

I watched the evening news and noticed a picture of some men swimming in the ocean. I called my father and told him to come see what was happening. My parents walked into the living room. My father told me those people were Mexicans who were trying to come to America.

During the newscast, there was also a picture of two trailer trucks. When the police officer opened up the backs of the trucks, we saw a lot of Mexicans inside. Some had died. There was also an incident showing a police officer beating an individual. My father said, "Now they're whipping on those poor little Mexicans." Shortly after that, my mother told us she had always wanted to be a defense lawyer.

I looked up at my parents and said, "I want to be a lawyer when I grow up."

The apartment my family and I lived in was kind of small. At one time, there were at least six of us living there. We were decent people and were a close-knit family.

My relatives spent a lot of time with us during the Christmas holiday season. My mother prepared dinner for everyone on Christmas Day. The meal included a turkey and dressing, macaroni and cheese, sweet potatoes, greens, potato salad and cranberry sauce. Two weeks before Christmas, my mother would go to the store and pick out a lot of toys for me and my brother. On Christmas Eve, after we had gone to bed, my parents would bring a large box of toys into the apartment. I found out what they were doing when I woke up and I saw the large box by the front door. I assumed that they hid the toys in their bedroom until they knew that we were asleep and then they would put the presents under the Christmas Tree. On Christmas Day we would get up early and open our presents. My parents tried to buy us every toy we wanted.

After living there for approximately four years, we grew tired of the small space—and the pests. The management company could not get rid of the roaches and mice that came out after dark. One night I went to the kitchen for a glass of water and saw a mouse sitting in the middle of the hallway leading to the kitchen.

My parents were very upset about the rodent problem. One day, my mother went into the closet to get some clothes for me to wear to school and saw a mouse jump out of a bag on the floor. It ran into the next room. My father put down mouse traps to catch them. Every month, my father told us he would speak to someone at the management company the next time he paid the rent.

Both my parents worked and my grandmother lived with us for a while. I really enjoyed having her around after school. She had an associate's degree in science. She would always instill in us the value of an education. I enjoyed going to school, and my grandmother would help me with my homework. I made good grades. One year, I even got a promotion from kindergarten to second grade, skipping first grade.

After a couple of years, the neighborhood started changing. There did not seem to be any bad kids in the neighborhood, but things were changing. For example, one day after school, my grandmother and I were looking out the window and saw a young mother walking down the street holding her son by his jacket and hitting him with her fist. She kept asking him, "Where is the kid who took my gun away from you?" This continued all the way down the block.

My grandmother and I looked at each other, and she said, "That's awful."

There was one kid everyone called the neighborhood bully. On Saturdays my brother and I took piano lessons at a neighbor's house. One Saturday we decided to skip piano lessons and take a walk down Fifty-First Street. We were approximately two blocks from home when we encountered this bully. He stopped us, took the can of pop he was holding, and poured half of it on top of my head before he let us pass. He was really mean, and no one wanted to fight him. (This happened during the summertime, so at least my hair dried pretty fast.)

Later during the year, my grandmother moved into her own apartment. My uncle Henry and aunt Louise lived a block away, so my mother would let us stay at their place after school so we wouldn't be alone.

My parents were constantly saying how they wanted to save enough money to buy a house. Eventually, my father spoke to someone at the real-estate office. When he came home one Friday evening after delivering the rent, he told us he had spoken to someone regarding the problem with the rodents. He told the manager that the rent was steadily going up, but the building was deteriorating and was becoming infested with mice. My father told us the manager told him, "You just happen to be one of those unfortunate individuals." My father told us he thought he may be poor, but he did not consider himself an unfortunate individual.

After a couple of years, my parents saved enough money for a down payment on a house. We moved into a two-apartment building on the southeast side of Chicago. My aunt and uncle, who lived on Fifty-First Street, decided it was time for them to move too. They moved to the southeast side with us. We lived on the second floor, and my aunt, uncle, and cousins lived on the first floor.

All of us were very excited about moving into our new residence. The neighborhood was very nice. I remember my father saying you could hear a pin drop at ten o 'clock at night. There were still some white people living in the area, but they were selling their homes as fast as they could. When I was young, I enjoyed sitting on my front porch or playing in the backyard. My grandmother would spend the weekend with us whenever she could, and sometimes my mother allowed me to get on the CTA (Chicago Transit Authority) bus to visit her.

Our house was a lot bigger than the apartment we used to rent, and we loved the space. There was a living room, a sitting room, three bedrooms, a dining room, and a kitchen. We had an enclosed sun porch. There was a basement, but it was not furnished. We did have a washing machine. It was one of the first ones manufactured. You had to put the clothes through the rollers by turning the knob on the side. This was the way you wrung the water out of your clothes. After a couple of years, my mother was able to purchase a clothes dryer. We also bought a ping pong table to put in the basement.

There were a lot of stores in the neighborhood. There was an Allendale Furniture store on Seventy-Ninth Street. It was a beautiful store, almost a block long, and they only sold French provincial furniture. One day I went to the store with my mother to pick out a sectional sofa for our living room. The sofa was an off-white color. It was very elegant-looking. Unfortunately, the sofa I picked out was too big for our living room. My mother had to take the center piece out and put it on one side of the living room and the two end pieces of the sofa on the other side. The sofa still looked nice there.

There were a couple of department stores, a hat shop, restaurants, dry cleaners, grocery stores, jewelry stores, and a couple of taverns in the neighborhood. There was also a funeral home, a theater, and a Walgreens drug store. I thought this store was really nice because you could buy a number of things for the house, as well as fill prescription drugs.

In the 1970s, some Walgreens had a lunch counter. You could sit and eat a hamburger and french fries and a number of different meals.

When I was sixteen, I went to the jewelry store to price some of the items. I told the salesperson I liked a lot of the gold chains, but I couldn't afford any of them because they were a little expensive. The salesperson, who was also part owner of the store, was very nice to me. He told me he would give me one of the gold chains. He selected a twelve-inch chain with a pendant on it. I thought it was really nice. I went home and showed it to my mother.

I wasn't too surprised when she told me I couldn't keep it. I was only sixteen, and I knew that my mother would not allow me to keep a gift from a man. I believe that my mother was suspicious of the salesperson's intentions. She told me to go back to the store and give it back to the person who gave it to me. She also instructed me to stay out of the jewelry store.

The next day, I took the necklace back to the jewelry store and I told the salesperson that my mother would not let me keep it. The salesperson told me that that was okay and I said goodbye and I left the store.

One summer my mother and my aunt Shirley took my brother, Michael, and me to Spring Valley Resorts for a vacation. There was a swimming pool at the cabin we were staying in. It was around eighty-five degrees outside, and my brother and I wanted to go swimming. We asked my mother if we could go. She told us we did not know how to swim. We told her we had learned when we were in day camp. Finally she told us we could go swimming. My brother knew how to swim. I could swim a little, but I had not learned how to tread water. (I had tried to learn at day camp but just couldn't do it.)

My brother ran ahead. By the time I reached the pool, I could see him at the far end of it. I ran over to him. He was standing on a ledge around the inside of the pool. I just assumed he was in the shallow end. I climbed down the ladder to get in. I did not notice the diving board at the end and never asked him how deep the water was. I stepped off the ladder and into the pool.

I panicked as I began to sink. My only thought was that you come up for air three times before you drown. When I came up for air the second time, I could see my brother swimming toward me. The third time I came up for air, I saw a man diving into the pool to save me.

After I got out, I thanked the man for saving my life. I asked my brother if he was okay. He told me he was, but he did not want to go back in the pool.

When we returned to the cabin, I told my mother how I almost drowned and a white man dived into the pool and pulled me out.

We stayed in Spring Valley for a week, but we didn't go back to the pool. We went sightseeing, and we took a ride on the river on an amphibious duck boat. I really enjoyed our vacation.

Once we returned home, things were back to normal. I spent the rest of my summer playing with some of the kids on my block.

One Saturday afternoon, my mother told me my cousin Nicole, who lived on the first floor, was sick and the doctor was coming to the house to examine her. My mother told me I should let the doctor examine me too, so I went downstairs to see the doctor. I was eleven years old. My aunt was with me when the doctor examined me in my cousin's bedroom. To my dismay, the doctor told me I had pneumonia and he wanted to admit me to the hospital the same day. I wondered how it was possible for me to have pneumonia. I did not have any signs of having a cold. My eyes were not watery, my nose was not running, and I wasn't coughing. I was not feeling fatigued and didn't have a fever or chills. I was doing the things any other child would be doing at age eleven.

My mother came downstairs to speak to the doctor. He told her I had pneumonia and he wanted her to take me to Hopkins Memorial Hospital. In 1967, black people were not allowed admittance into some hospitals on the South Side of Chicago. To be perfectly honest, a couple of hospitals there wouldn't even allow black people to receive treatment in their emergency rooms. After my mother spoke to the doctor, we went upstairs, and she helped me pack some things to take to the hospital.

After being admitted, my parents and I met with Dr. Bartley, my primary-care doctor. He had previously ordered a set of chest X-rays. While looking at the X-rays, he pointed to an area behind my rib cage on the right side and told us that was where my enlarged thymus gland was located.

My mother and father indicated they could see what he was talking about, but I continued to ask him where was the thymus gland located because I did not see anything at all on the X-ray.

The next day I met Dr. Nichols, who was a pediatrician. He was an elderly man with white hair. I really liked him. He asked me why

I was in the hospital. I told him I had pneumonia and an enlarged thymus gland. He came to my room to see me a couple of times, but he sort of pulled away from me. I assumed he wanted nothing to do with the situation. One day when Dr. Nichols came to see how I was doing, I asked him when I would be able to go home.

Dr. Nichols replied, "You can go home today."

I called my parents and told them the doctor was releasing me from the hospital. When my parents arrived with my clothes to take me home, Dr. Bartley came into the room. He raised his voice and asked me, "Who told you that you could go home?"

My father pulled him to the side and told him I was just a child and he should not speak to me in that manner. I ended up staying in the hospital.

After a few days, Dr. Bartley informed me I would have to undergo exploratory surgery. He told me the surgeon would make a small incision under my neck and insert a scope to look in my chest. During the same week, I was moved to another room, and the doctor put me under an oxygen tent to help with my breathing. I do not recall having a problem with my breathing.

The next week, I asked Dr. Bartley, "How long do I have to stay in the hospital?" He told me he was not sure. He also told me there was a school upstairs if I wanted to go to school while I was there. I went because I did not want to fall behind in my schoolwork. A week later, I had the exploratory surgery.

A couple of weeks after the exploratory surgery, the surgeon, Dr. Newman, performed surgery on my chest. The surgeon had to split my chest bone to remove the thymus gland.

He also made two smaller incisions, one on the left and one on the right side, just below my rib cage, to drain the fluid from my chest.

Approximately one month later, the doctor released me from the hospital. He explained to me and my parents that the enlarged thymus gland is called a thymoma, a rare, usually benign tumor arising from thymus tissue. I have always felt the surgery was unnecessary, and I even told myself I would file a civil suit once I turned eighteen.

I was brought up in a Christian home and went to church just about every Sunday. I graduated from a Catholic grammar school. In my graduation book, my grandmother wrote a quote that I will always remember: "Reach for the moon, but if you should happen to fall among the stars, be the best of whatever you are."

After grammar school, I went to a public high school, and I made good grades. I even enrolled in an advanced placement college course. During my junior year, I reminded my parents that I was still interested in becoming a lawyer. They probably thought I was chasing a dream. All across the United States in the 1960s and '70s, a lot of black people were not admitted into law schools or medical schools. The only other reason I felt my parents were probably reluctant about discussing law school with me was because of the surgical scar on my chest. I don't know why, but at that time it seemed to be taboo for a woman to wear a blouse that was buttoned all the way up to the top.

My father told me I would have to go to school for seven years, and my mother made no comment at all. I graduated from high school at the age of seventeen and really wanted to go away to college.

My mother told me I could go away to school if I received a scholarship. I ranked fifth, at the top of my senior class, but I did not receive a scholarship. Perhaps I should have spoken to a counselor about a scholarship before graduation.

I wasn't ashamed of the scar on my chest. As previously stated, I felt the surgery was unnecessary. During the summer months I would wear halter tops and sundresses, just like all the other young ladies in the 1970s.

During my early twenties, I had to go to the doctor on several occasions for a cold or for a regular checkup. I began to sense that something was wrong because the doctor would examine me and say, "What is that scar on your chest?" Each time I would tell the doctor about the surgery that I had when I was eleven.

Apparently, the thymus gland is supposed to shrink by puberty, but Dr. Bartley told me that my thymus gland was enlarged. After doing some research on my own, approximately twenty years after the surgery, I discovered the thymus gland is located underneath the neck and not the bottom of the rib cage.

In the late 1970s, the neighborhood was beginning to change. A lot of the stores were going out of business or simply leaving the neighborhood. The grocery store closed. The Allendale Furniture Store closed, and the state of Illinois opened up a public aid office in the building where the furniture store used to be.

The Madison Theater closed. I went to see a movie at the theater once, but a few years after that I was told by some friends that the theater was not being kept up and it was infested with rodents.

The block I lived on was pretty stable. Just about all the families bought their homes around the same time. My family and I knew almost everyone. We would have a block party every year. All of the homeowners would move their cars off of the street before nine in the morning, and then some of the men would put wooden horses at each end of the street to stop traffic from entering.

Next, they would set up approximately six to eight tables. There was food and beverages on each one. Everyone would go from one table to the next to sample the food, desserts, and drinks. We would hire a disc jockey to play music. The adults and children would dance and have fun in the street. The party usually lasted until four or five in the morning.

One year everyone on the block decided to have matching light poles installed on their front lawns, which were well manicured. The poles made the block look nicer, and we had plenty of light. The one or two streetlights run by the city were not enough.

Everyone on the block was friendly. There was one couple who had six kids, four boys and two girls. For some reason, the oldest son was an was incorrigible child. I believe he started stealing items from the local stores at the age of ten and was sent to the juvenile detention center when he was thirteen or fourteen. This sort of baffled me because I knew he came from a good family.

During the 1970s, a lot of boys were being expelled from school, or they dropped out. This was happening all over Chicago—the east side, South Side, and the west side. I was a teenager at the time, but I knew this type of situation would only lead to trouble for these young men. They would hang out on street corners, and eventually a lot of them joined a gang. We did not have a problem with gangs before I moved from the southeast side of Chicago, but I had heard about them in other areas of the city.

I could tell that my neighborhood was changing. A lot of young boys in the neighborhood who no longer attended school seemed to lose hope about anything positive happening to them in the future. They didn't seem to care about themselves anymore.

This is how the gang situation starts, and people don't appear to take an interest in their communities anymore. A lot of these young boys begin to commit crimes, such as burglaries and robberies, in their own communities. I feel that most people are reluctant to become involved and refuse to report individuals to the police. The gang member may be the young man from across the street or the neighbor's son who lives next door.

When there is a gang in the community, shootings and drug deals take place. A lot of people, including the parents of these individuals, just lose all hope. People begin to change, and property values begin to depreciate.

Even though a large number of young boys were being expelled from school or dropped out, they still needed to be educated. These boys were all under the age of eighteen. Someone should have placed them in an alternative school, or if they were in high school when they stopped attending school, the school administrators or their parents should have insisted they get their GED. Everyone eighteen years or older should have a diploma or GED. Without one, these young men would not get the opportunity to go to college. These young boys needed to attend school in order to learn some skills to prepare them for the workforce.

Living in Chicago was okay, but there were problems between the citizens in the communities and the Chicago police department. My father told me about an incident that happened to him shortly after he moved to Chicago. He told me a police officer had stopped him for a traffic violation. After the officer ran a check on his driver's license, he returned to the car and asked him if he had ever been arrested. My father told him no. The officer replied, "You are not an American citizen if you've never been arrested." The police officer gave my father a warning and that was the end of it. My father came home and told us about the incident.

During the 1970s, an encounter between a black man and a Chicago police officer was often volatile. The officers would beat a black man with a nightstick if the black man didn't answer a question the way the officer wanted him to.

An incident most Chicagoans will probably never forget is when the Chicago police department went to the home of the Black Panthers Party and shot and killed everyone there while they were sleeping.

I know we cannot always believe everything we read in the newspaper, but I have been told the apartment building where they were killed looked like a war zone. There were bullet holes everywhere.

I was a teenager at the time, but I remember reading an article in the newspaper before the shooting that stated people in the Black Panther Party were carrying guns and trying to monitor the Chicago police because they were constantly beating black men in the street and at the police stations. I don't believe killing everyone in the Black Panther Party was the way to resolve the problems between the Chicago police department and the black community.

After graduating from high school, I went to a junior college. I thought I would never go to law school because I had no one to guide me and tell me what classes I should take, although I knew that it would probably be a good idea to major in history or political science. Believe it or not, in 1973, I knew that computers would be the most profitable business in the future, but I could not wrap my mind around the idea of majoring in computer programming. During my second semester, I decided to drop out of school and find a job so I could earn enough money to get my own apartment.

Chapter 2

My First Job

In the mid-1970s I found my first job. I went to work as a secretary for a nonprofit social-service agency on the Southside of Chicago. During my time there, I got a chance to learn about some of the problems that plagued our neighborhoods. The social workers were constantly busy trying to resolve problems for the families on their caseloads.

While working at the nonprofit, I decided I wanted to find an apartment. Eventually, I found one on 107th Street in the Roseland Community and lived there about a year.

At that time the area was nice. I never had any problems with the people in the community. If there was a gang problem, I did not know about it. There were times when I would feel hungry late in the evening and would order barbecue wings from the rib house down the street. I would go there any time during the day or evening and never saw any group of young men doing anything wrong. I certainly do not recall hearing any gunshots. I did not have a car at the time, so I would walk or catch a bus whenever I wanted to go somewhere. When I returned home a little late after being out with a couple of my girlfriends, I was not afraid to walk half a block to my apartment.

I decided to move back to my parents' home before starting my next job.

After I left my job at the agency, I went to work for a large engineering firm in downtown Chicago. Engineers and draftsmen worked there. Three ladies, including me, worked in the secretarial pool. It was my first job as a word processor. Lisa was the vice president's secretary, and the other secretary and I typed documents for everyone else at the firm. The three of us became good friends. Lisa was married and had two kids. Jackie and I were also married, but we did not have any kids. Sometimes Jackie and I would go to a restaurant after work for dinner and a couple of drinks. Jackie was married to a guy named Michael. They were very nice people. They lived in an apartment building on the north side of Chicago.

Some weekends, my husband and I would go to visit them, and we would listen to music, eat dinner, and play bid whist (a card game) for three or four hours. Jackie and I remained friends for a long time.

One Friday evening we decided to go to Boka Restaurant for dinner. While we were eating, I asked her "why is it that Lisa does not spend any time with us after work?"

Jackie told me about Lisa's husband, John. At the time, Lisa and John were living in the South Shore area. Jackie told me Lisa and John enjoyed spending time with their family and friends.

I worked at the engineering firm for approximately two years. During this time, my husband and I divorced and I moved back home with my parents.

When I was twenty-one, I had my first child. A couple of years later, my parents decided the house we were living in was becoming a little too cramped. My aunt and uncle also decided it was time to start looking for a home of their own. They ended up buying a bungalow house on the northeast side of Chicago.

On weekends I would go with my parents to look for a house. We looked as far south as 147th Street. My father was driving down Halsted Street when he told me that he remembered when a black person was not allowed to even walk through Danville Park. Well, we had finally gotten to the point where black people could not only walk through Danville Park, we could buy homes there. There were some really nice homes there. I saw one home on the corner that I really liked. Unfortunately, the house was not for sale. (It was on the corner, and it probably cost a lot more than my parents could afford anyway.)

At the time, white people were moving out of Danville Park, but there were still a few who stayed. Sometimes I believe they stayed because they were older and did not want to move.

After looking for a house for a couple of months, my parents finally decided on one that was next to a corner house. The homes on the corner were really large. The homes extended from the corner to the alley. The homes were approximately forty-five to fifty feet long.

Our house was a three-bedroom with a finished basement. We had an above-ground swimming pool in the backyard that we used for years. A few years after we moved into the house, my father decided to put a pool table in the basement, which we used for recreation.

My mother had a different attitude. She felt that we should stop shouting whenever we were in the house. Sometimes the people in our family spoke a little loudly. One day I was in the bedroom and my mother was in the kitchen cooking, and I called out to her to ask her a question. She came running from the kitchen, through the living room, and into my bedroom to tell me I will not be yelling or calling out to her from one room to another. I am sure she meant we were not going to have our neighbors thinking we did not know how to live a quiet suburban lifestyle.

It may not seem like a lot to most people, but it was home. I have always felt that black people should have a decent place to live, good-paying jobs, and good schools.

My next job interview was downtown at an insurance company. When I went to the personnel office, a white man in his early forties sat down to interview me. During the interview, I was thinking that I would love to be a personnel manager.

My afterthought was, *Who am I kidding? This is 1979.* I did not know if white people would allow a black person to be a personnel manager, someone who would hire and fire their employees. I did not get the job, but I had a different idea about the type of job I wanted.

I went on several interviews that week. Approximately two weeks later I received a call from Tammy, the supervisor at MetLife Insurance Co. She asked if I wanted a job as a legal secretary. I told her yes, and I started work the following week. I was the secretary for two paralegals and two attorneys. I met some very nice people while working there.

I became friends with a couple of people. Carolyn worked in the accounting department, and Patricia was a graphic artist. The three of us became good friends.

The attorneys I worked for were pleasant. At times I would look at them and think it would be great to be in their positions. They probably had big salaries, families, and lived in large homes in the suburbs.

Tammy was my immediate supervisor. One day she and I decided to go to a Chinese restaurant. During lunch we talked about where we lived, and she told me that she lived in Danville Park. I told her I also lived there as well. Coincidentally, we lived approximately six blocks from each other. I thought it was great we lived in the same community. She and her husband were expecting their first baby.

I don't know if she and her husband ever moved out of the neighborhood, but I certainly hope not. I am a firm believer in integration, but unfortunately, during the 1960s, '70s, and '80s, most white people moved out if black people were moving in.

In 1981 I was hired by New Data Computer Consulting Firm, located in downtown Chicago. My title was secretary/word processor. My responsibilities included typing, accounts payables/receivables, payroll, and making airline reservation. I also had the responsibility of picking up documents from prospective clients and delivering completed computer-programming documents to our clients once the project was finished. The time I spent outside the office really made my job seem even more worthwhile. The area I worked in was contemporary and spacious. I had to type for approximately thirty people. The staff was diversified. Many employees came from other countries.

When it was time to hire another secretary, I had to hire someone. I interviewed at least four or five people. All of them were qualified for the position. The person I decided to hire was a young lady named Leslie, who was from Nicaragua. She and I were good coworkers.

Leslie's husband was also from Nicaragua. He worked for a catering company in the downtown area. He sometimes stopped by the office to hello.

About a year after I started working for the firm, our company merged with DataPro Computer Consulting Company, and we move into a bigger office space in the downtown area. Sharon, the company manager, hired an interior designer to set up the cubicles and offices for the employees. All of us had the same job descriptions; we simply worked for different people.

On the weekends I spend my time bowling and horseback riding. A few of my friends and I would go see a movie and go out to dinner afterward.

There seemed to be a void in my life. I wanted to do something else in my spare time. I decided to enroll in a computer programming class. In the beginning, I did not know if it was something that would hold my interest. Jerry, the president of DataPro Computer Consulting Company, told me that after I finished school, I would have a job as a computer programmer at his company. But after I finished the class, I decided my interest was not in computer programming.

At work, some of the guys would take time out of their schedules to talk to me about their personal lives—and they had some pretty interesting lives.

For instance, there was one computer analyst who lived in the downtown area. I believe he lived a comfortable lifestyle because of where he lived. (In the 1980s some condominiums in the downtown area were very expensive.)

The computer programmers there were mostly men. We had a couple of women who were also programmers. I overheard a couple of the guys talking about one of the ladies. He said she was a rich, spoiled little brat from New York. I thought she was a terrific person.

When I worked downtown, I noticed a lot of women wore full-length mink coats to work during the winter months. At that time, in the 1980s, black women were just beginning to wear fur coats. There was a time when a black person would lose his or her job for trying to "act like a white person." Years ago, if a black person drove a new car or wore a full-length mink coat to work, he or she would lose his or her job for "acting white."

I enjoyed talking to Brian, a computer analyst. He was young, good looking, and soft spoken. One day he told me he was preparing to attend his cousin's wedding in Germany. I asked him if he thought the Mercedes Benz is cheaper there. He said they are cheaper in Germany. I could not afford a Mercedes Benz, but I have always thought they were good looking and dependable cars. Believe it or not, when Brian returned from Germany, he told me that he had bought a Mercedes Benz while he was in Germany and he had it shipped back here to the United States.

To be honest, I'm sure some people would be a little envious of the people I worked with and their lifestyles. I am not a jealous or envious person, but I wished I could have lived like some of the people I worked with.

After working for the company for a couple of years, Sharon, my manager, decided to ask Jerry, the company president, if he would give me the title of supervisor along with a raise. Jerry did not feel it was necessary for me to have the title of supervisor, because I did not have enough people to supervise. Leslie, the other secretary/word processor, worked directly with the computer programmers and analysts. She and I worked independently. I did not get a new title, but I did get the raise, which was good.

In 1984, a friend of mine told me JDT's Magazine Distribution Company on the Southside of Chicago was hiring. I went to take a written exam. Three months later I received a letter letting me know I had passed the test with a score of ninety-four.

In the latter part of 1984 I received another letter from one of their offices. The letter stated that I had to pass a physical test, which required some light lifting. I also had to pass a test on the computer in order to complete the job requirements. I was given a date and time to take the tests. I went to the facility on a Tuesday afternoon. The tests took approximately two hours.

After passing, I was offered the job the same day. I accepted the offer after being told what my salary would be.

The next day I went back to my old job. I spent most of the day trying to think of a reason for quitting. Finally, I went into Sharon's office and told her I had to quit because I had a sick parent at home who I had to take care of. I did not think my manager would be willing to give me a three-dollar-an-hour increase, which is what the new job was paying. Instead of making nine dollars an hour, I would be making twelve. Also, I wanted to take the new job because it was closer to home, and I would not have to take a bus and a train to get to work each day. I had bought a used car to drive to the bus stop when I started working for DataPro Computer Consulting Company. Now, I will be able to drive to work and back.

During the day, all the guys stopped by my desk to say good-bye. I enjoyed working with everyone at the computer consulting firm.

Sharon told me she was sorry I had to leave. I worked a full day.

The following Monday, I started my new job. Besides the fact that I was making more money, my working hours were 8:00 p.m. to 4:30 a.m. This was good for me because I was able to take my son to school in the morning, pick him up from school in the afternoon, and spend some quality time with him before taking him to the babysitter after dinner. I kept this work schedule for a couple of years before I requested an earlier starting time.

Usually, you had to have at least three years seniority before you can bid on an earlier starting time.

In 1986 I decided it was again time for me to move out of my parents' house. I found an apartment in the south suburbs. The location was ideal because my apartment was approximately three blocks from my son's school. Shortly after moving into my new apartment, I decided it was time for me to buy a new car. I went to several different dealerships and test drove several different makes and models before finally deciding to buy a foreign car.

Life seemed pretty good. I had a decent-paying job, a nice apartment, and a new car. My son and I spent weekends doing things we enjoyed. He and I were just beginning to learn to roller skate.

My son is an only child, and I knew he would enjoy the company of another kid on the weekends, so we would drive to Chicago to pick up my nephew and his mother, and they would spend the weekend at my place. All of us would go bowling, horseback riding, or out to dinner. There was a great pizza place down the street from my apartment. We usually ate there on Saturdays. On Sunday evening, we would drive my nephew and his mother back to Chicago.

At work, I was spending approximately six hours a day on the computer. There were times when I wanted to quit my job. My back was beginning to hurt because I sat at the computer for a long period of time. Also, I did not like the color of the screen. I started complaining to my supervisor. I told her it was beginning to have an adverse affect on my eyes.

There were some other positions where I could sort the magazines or repair magazines that had been damaged. The only problem was that you had to start work at 2:00 p.m. This was a problem for me because my son did not get out of school until 3:00 p.m., and I did not have anyone who could pick him up from school and take him to the babysitter.

I continued to work on the old computer.

During the summer months, I enrolled my son in a day-camp program where he learned how to swim. Naturally, I wanted to be a good swimmer too. I decided to take a swimming class so I could learn to tread water.

One day during the swimming class, a couple of ladies, the instructor, and I were swimming in the deep end of the pool. The instructor was teaching us how to tread water. At one point, we decided to see just how long we could hold our breath underwater. I don't know what came over the instructor, but she had her hand on my head, and I felt like I had to force my head up in order to come up for air. I assumed that she wanted me to try and hold my breath for a long period of time, but I had held my breath long enough. The incident seemed to frighten her a little. I don't believe that she was trying to drown me. I did not report the incident to anyone. I believe she decided to quit her job because the following week, we had a new instructor. I finished the swim class and finally learned how to tread water.

I also enjoyed going to the sandwich shop on the corner near my apartment. One evening, my son and I were in the shop when two of his day-camp instructors walked in. One was black and one was white. We started talking about how my son was doing at camp, and I asked how they happened to become instructors. One told me he had just graduated from college and was going to be a schoolteacher in the fall. The other instructor told me he was a schoolteacher and was working on getting his master's degree.

I was impressed with them and congratulated them on their accomplishments. While I was standing there waiting for my sandwich, I kept thinking about their accomplishments. I said to myself, *I wish I could have been a college graduate.* My second thought was, how could I possibly do what they have done? *Here I am, almost thirty years old. How can I go to the junior college in Chicago and pick up my transcript and start going to college again?* I felt sad and told myself it was too late for me to start going to school again. But this feeling inside me made me realize I would be a much happier person if I had a college degree.

After I paid for our sandwiches, I told my son's day-camp instructors good-bye, and we went home.

It was 1986, and summer was going by pretty fast. We still had some eighty- and ninety-degree temperatures in August. Since I worked in the evenings, sometimes I would take a nap during the day. I lived on the third floor, so I felt it would be okay to leave the balcony window open while I was sleeping. It certainly saved me money on my electric bill because I did not keep the air conditioner on in the morning or early afternoon. Did I ever get the shock of my life.

One day I woke up and went into the living room to close the balcony window and turn on the air conditioner. I noticed a neat little pile of charcoal on the left side of the balcony. I did not own a barbecue grill, so the charcoal did not belong to me.

My first thought was that someone had stood up on the rail on the balcony underneath mine and placed the charcoal on my balcony. The couple who lived underneath me were nice people with three kids. The husband worked, and his wife stayed home and took care of the kids. On weekends, they would invite their family or friends to come over, and they would cook on the grill.

After looking down, I realized there was no way he could have dumped those briquettes on my balcony. My next thought was that the maintenance guys must have put a ladder up to my balcony and placed the charcoal there. There was a management office on the apartment complex, but I did not think it was necessary to ask them if they knew anything about it. From that day forth, I never slept with the balcony window open. I never found out who placed the charcoal on my balcony.

I met some nice people while I was living there. One couple, Marilyn and Anthony, had just moved here from the south. Marilyn told me she was born and raised in Alabama. This couple had three kids, and her youngest son and mine played together quite often.

After a couple of years, Marilyn and John decided to buy a house. One day my son and I went to visit Marilyn, her husband, and the kids. While she and I were sitting in the living room, she told me she was tired of being at home all day with the kids. She told me she wanted to look for a job. She also said she had enrolled at a junior college and her classes would begin the following week. I told her I was happy for her. She and I were approximately the same age. I was glad to see she was up to the challenge and excited about going to school.

Marilyn had fixed a delicious dinner for us. We ate and all sat and talked for a couple of hours. Afterward, my son and I went home.

The next day, I told myself, *If Marilyn can do it, I can do it.* I picked up the telephone and called the registrar's office at the college I had previously attended in Chicago, and I told the person who answered that I needed a copy of my college transcript. She said she would mail a copy to the college of my choice, but I had to pick up a copy, which was already in an envelope with a special seal on it to take to the college.

Two days later I went to Chicago and picked up the transcript. I took it to the junior college where I enrolled for classes. My classes started in the fall. I would be going to school during the day and working in the evening. Ms. Smith, my supervisor, was still giving me a hard time at work. I was constantly telling her I did not think working on the type of computer I had to work on was good for my eyes.

Finally, I went to the manager and asked if he had a position open for a supervisor. He told me he would think about it and let me know. About a week later, he contacted me and said I could start working as a supervisor the next day.

The next day when I went to work, I reported to the manager's office. He instructed one of his supervisors to train me in different areas on the workroom floor. After my training, I supervised approximately twenty to thirty employees for six months. At the end of the six months, there were two or three other people who wanted to be supervisors. I had to go back to my job as a computer operator. My manager allowed me to work as a supervisor for six months, but I knew when I accepted the position, that it would be temporary.

In 1990 I was still working on the old computer. One day I decided to speak to someone in the human resources department. The gentleman I spoke to told me I would have to bring some documentation from my doctor stating why I could not work on that computer. At one point during our conversation, I told him I was considering resigning. He told me not to quit but to continue to work and bring in documentation.

The next week I went to see my doctor, who wasn't just a medical doctor was also a surgeon. I told him about the effect that the computer was having on my eyes. He instructed me to go to Hopkins Memorial Hospital and sign a release of information form so I could get all my medical information, which included everything about the surgery I'd had when I was eleven years old.

The following week, the person in medical records told me it would take about an hour for someone to copy all the documents. I waited while they were being copied.

I then took them home so I could read them. The stack of papers was about an inch thick. I read almost half the information before I got to the part about my surgery. When I read that part, I became a little upset. The report stated the tumor was wrapped around the phrenic nerves (nerves that originate in the neck and pass down between the lung and heart to reach the diaphragm) on the left and the right. In my opinion, this sounded totally ridiculous. I thought that it was strange when I read that the tumor was wrapped around the phrenic nerve on the left and the phrenic nerve on the right. I really did not think the surgery was necessary, and I wondered why I did not go ahead and sue the doctors and the hospital when I was eighteen. Let's not forget that the doctor indicated that the thymus gland is located in the area on the right side behind the rib cage. The next day I made an appointment to see my doctor.

I brought all my medical information to the doctor's office. After he finished reading the documents, I asked him if the surgery was necessary. He kind of dropped his head and said, "Yes, the surgery was necessary." It sounded almost as if he had mumbled under his breath.

I did not believe him because of his body language and the tone of his voice.

The next day I called several different attorneys to inquire about filing a medical malpractice lawsuit. One attorney told me I should have filed the lawsuit when I was eighteen. I could not believe I could not find an attorney willing to try to get my case into court. I was still upset about the surgery.

When I returned to work, I made an extra copy of my medical information and took it to the Human Resources department.

After a couple of weeks, someone from HR told me I could work in the magazine section until further notice.

For the next five years I worked in the magazine section. On several occasions, Ms. Smith, my supervisor, would come to my work area and ask if I could work on the computer because someone did not show up for work that day and she needed someone to fill in. I would work on the computer, but it was not on a regular basis. I was still thinking about my doctor's reaction to my medical information. Also, I was wondering, how do you unwrap part of a tumor from a phrenic nerve without damaging the nerve?

After giving my situation a lot of thought, I decided to file a civil lawsuit on my own. I wrote up the complaint and went downtown to the courthouse and paid the fee to file my complaint. After an hour waiting, my name was called. A young man named Robert asked me if he could speak to me for a few minutes. He told me he had read my complaint, and he also told me there was no way the judge would hear my case. I knew I should have filed the lawsuit when I was eighteen. I asked Robert if he could think of something, anything at all, to get my case into court. I told him I did not feel the surgery was necessary and surely, the statute of limitations could start again because I felt that filling a lawsuit at eighteen is not something most teenagers think about.

Robert told me I could go across the street to another courthouse to see if I could file my complaint there. I told him it did not make sense for me to go to another courthouse and pay an additional fee to file a complaint so that someone could tell me the same thing.

I left there feeling disappointed. It was around eleven thirty when I decided to grab lunch. After lunch, I bought a newspaper and boarded the train to go home.

At home I put all my medical documentation on a shelf, and the papers remained there for about three months before I decided to throw them away. The time had come and gone for me to file a lawsuit. At this point, there was nothing more that I could do, but I will always believe the surgery was unnecessary.

The next day I went to work feeling as if some things just happen in life whether they are right or wrong, but if you don't act in a timely manner to address the issue, no one seems to care about your dilemma.

I continued to work in the magazine section. My supervisor finally stopped asking me to work on the computer.

Chapter 3

Job Relocation

In the summer of 1991, the president of the company held a town-hall meeting at the job. He informed us that the company was moving to a new building in the southwest suburbs. He told us a small number of employees at the Southside location would remain there for one year. At the end of that period, they would have to commute to the new building. He also told us that if we decided to move closer to our place of employment, the company would pay for our moving expenses.

In September 1992 I started work in the new building. Fortunately, I was able to get a position working in the magazine section. My work schedule was 8:00 a.m. to 4:30 p.m. This worked out fine for me, although I had to get up early to drive forty miles to get to my job at eight. The new building was modern, and I enjoyed working there.

Everything seemed to be going well for me. I was working during the day and going to school in the evenings. About six months after I started working at the new building, I heard rumors about some other employees being dissatisfied with working on the old computers.

Even though the company had moved into a new building, we still had the same old computers. There was only one computer in the area where I worked, and I'm glad I didn't have to use it for very long. About three months after the rumors started, the old computers were replaced with new ones.

In December 1992 I started working with some of the clerks in the shipping department. It was my responsibility to make sure there were enough shipping labels in stock at all times. Our company shipped tons of magazines throughout the country and around the world.

I kept extra shipping labels in stock so anyone who needed them could go to the stock room and find the labels in my absence. My job was not very stressful. The nice part about it was that I got the opportunity to walk around most of the day.

About one year after I started working at the new location, I decided I should inquire about a better position. After all, I was attending school and majoring in business administration. I wanted to put some of the knowledge that I had acquired to good use. I called Mr. Tom Jenkins, the manager of the shipping department, to schedule a meeting with him. The next day he told me he was willing to let me become a supervisor. He said the position would last for a short period, and if I wanted to supervise on a regular basis, I would have to apply for the position whenever it was posted on the board.

The following week, Mr. Jenkins's secretary asked me to come up to the manager's office. When I walked in, the secretary handed me a sheet of paper with my new work schedule on it. I would start training the following week.

When I reported to work on Monday, I met with one of the supervisors who worked in shipping. She started training me in different areas on the workroom floor. After two weeks of training, I began supervising employees in the three sections that were assigned to me.

One year later, Mr. Jenkins left to take care of his ailing mother, and the company hired a new manager, Mr. Scott Stevens. My position as supervisor had ended a few months before Mr. Jenkins left the company. The day after Mr. Stevens started working for the company, he scheduled a meeting with all the employees. In one day he met with the employees who worked from 8:00 a.m. to 4:30 p.m. and the employees who worked from 4:00 p.m. to 12:30 a.m. Within the next couple of days, he scheduled a meeting with the employees who worked from 12:00 a.m. to 8:30 a.m. At these meetings, he would tell everyone what was expected as far as job performance. These meetings gave the employees a chance to voice their concerns or any complaints they might have.

Sometimes the meetings lasted as long as two hours. The time spent away from our work areas always seemed like a well-deserved break. If the meeting was in the morning, Mr. Stevens would make sure there was coffee and donuts for everyone. If the meeting was being held in the afternoon or late evening, there were different types of beverages and pizza for everyone. After the meeting, everyone had to return to their assignments.

During the first quarter of 1993, I decided I wanted to become an entry-level manager. One afternoon I went to Ms. Smith's office and asked her if I could become a manager.

Ordinarily, you have to be a supervisor before you can become a manager. I figured there shouldn't be a problem since I had worked as a supervisor in the past. Also, I was still attending school, and I knew that some of our supervisors were also in school.

For some reason, Ms. Smith did not want to go along with my request to become a manager. I knew some of the regular supervisors wouldn't like it because they'd had to apply for their positions and weren't able to bypass the supervisor position to become a manager. They did not want me to have a manager's position if it was not posted on the board and since I did not apply for it through the Human Resources department. Usually, if you are working as a manager, you may be in that position for a couple of years or longer.

After Ms. Smith told me she would not be able to grant my request, I decided to schedule a meeting with our manager, Mr. Stevens, to see if he would allow me to become a manager.

During my meeting with Mr. Stevens, he asked some questions about my prior experience as a supervisor and my educational background. Before the meeting ended, he asked for my phone number and said he would give me a call. I did not want to give Mr. Stevens my phone number. I told him that he could page me on the workroom floor, or he could call my supervisor and leave a message with her. A couple of weeks passed and I did not hear anything from Mr. Stevens.

At the end of the third week, I decided to contact the manager of Human Resources. I told her I had spoken to my supervisor and the president of the company about giving me the opportunity to become a manager. After talking to her for about twenty minutes, she told me she would look into the matter and call me back.

About a week later, Ms. Smith called me into her office. She told me the manager of Human Resources had contacted her and told her she could train me as a manager. Ms. Smith seemed to be a little upset because I contacted the Human Resource Manager. I really didn't care because I wanted to become a manager. I was very excited about the idea. The following week, Ms. Smith found someone to take my place on the workroom floor, and I began my training for the position of manager.

We had a supervisor's locker room and an employee locker room. I chose to keep my things in my locker in the employee's locker room. I had a good relationship with my coworkers and did not have problems with any of the ones I had previously supervised.

During the second week of my training, there was a problem. It was a Wednesday morning. When I arrived at work, I went to the employee locker room to put my things in my locker. A coworker named Maria was standing in front of her locker. I went to my locker, hung my coat up, and put my purse inside. Next, something unbelievable happened. While I was taking some papers off the top shelf of my locker, I accidentally dropped my pen on the floor. When I bent down to retrieve it, I felt something hit me on my arm. Maria had taken her bag and hit me on my arm with it. She quickly turned around and looked in the opposite direction. I gently touched her on her arm and asked her why she hit me. She turned around and put her finger in my face and told me "don't you touch me". At that point, I wanted to leave the locker room. Maria was blocking the aisle, so I could not walk past her to get to the door at the front of the locker room. I didn't think about the exit door, which was located at the end of the aisle and to the left. The exit door leads directly to the workroom floor.

I believe I was in a state of shock. I could not believe what had just happened. Instead of going to my supervisor's office, I walked to the nearest telephone on the workroom floor. I needed a minute to think about what had just happened. There had never been any other time when I had a reason to call the police to come to my place of employment to report an incident.

After ten or fifteen minutes, I decided that calling the police and reporting the incident would be the right thing to do. Before I could pick up the phone, the phone rang. Ms. Smith was on the other end of the phone. She told me she wanted to see me in her office.

When I walked into her office, I was surprised to see Mr. Stevens, Maria, the coworker who was in the locker room with me, two police officers, and a woman I had never seen before. Later I found out that her name was Lori Webber, she was a private investigator for the company. When Mr. Stevens got up to walk past me, he almost hit my leg. The police officer sort of reared up at him.

Mr. Stevens began to tell me that my coworker called him and said there had been an incident in the locker room. I told Mr. Stevens and the police officer exactly what had happened. I vehemently denied the allegations made by Maria. Afterwards, the police officer told me he was going to arrest me for battery. It was the middle of December, and I didn't want to go outside without my coat. I gave my locker key to Ms. Smith and asked her if she could bring me my coat and my purse. She brought my things to me.

Next, one of the officers smiled and asked the other officer, "Where are we going with this, Grundy or Livingston County?"

Before I left the office, Ms. Webber, the private investigator, told me she would meet me at the police station.

The officer did not put handcuffs on me. We walked outside and a police wagon was sitting in front of the building. I asked if I had to ride in there instead of in a squad car. We proceeded to walk around the police wagon, and he opened a small door on the side. I was surprised when the officer opened up the door. I saw a big leather seat. I got inside and rode to the police station.

I was glad the officer had allowed Ms. Smith to bring me my coat and purse. I had some money in my purse that I was planning to use to buy Christmas presents. I was hoping I could post bond for myself to get out of jail if the judge did not release me on my own recognizance.

Once we arrived at the police station, the officer parked in a garage and opened the door to let me out. Before entering the station, he took his gun and placed it in a black box near the door. After we walked inside, he spoke to a female officer named Rachael McGinnis.

Officer McGinnis asked me to have a seat. Once we started talking, I asked her if I would be going in front of the judge today. It was about two o'clock in the afternoon. She told me it was too late. Next, I asked her if I could post bond for myself. She told me that the bond was one thousand dollars and I needed one hundred dollars in order to post bond. I really wasn't sure why I had to pay a bond. I asked Officer McGinnis if I could be released on my own recognizance. Officer McGinnis stated that my coworker accused me of poking her on the arm and threatening her, neither of which I did. Officer McGinnis spoke to me for a few minutes, and during our conversation, she told me I had to be processed and fingerprinted. At that point I told her that I wanted to post bond. Luckily I had enough money in my purse.

I asked if I could sit in the chair next to the secretary's desk while she was doing her paperwork. At that time, there was a secretary who was sitting across from us. I assumed that she was typing something for the police officers who worked there. I looked to my left and I saw a man sitting in a small room with a blanket wrapped around his shoulders. I did not want Officer McGinnis to put me in a holding cell. Officer McGinnis told me to stay where I was at. Ten minutes later, Officer McGinnis came back to the desk where I was sitting and asked me to walk with her to the area where she had to take the fingerprints. After that we went back to the desk and the officer began filling out the form to process my bond.

Shortly afterwards, Ms. Webber, the investigator from my job walked in. She looked at me as if she did not appreciate the fact that I was sitting there at the desk. She probably expected me to be in a holding cell. She spoke to Officer McGinnis for a few minutes.

Ms. Webber told Officer McGinnis that she wanted to make a set of fingerprints. Officer McGinnis told her she had already taken a set of prints and would mail her a copy. Ms. Webber told the officer she wanted to make her own set of fingerprints for her file.

She and I went back to the area the officers use to take fingerprints. Ms. Webber made a set of fingerprints with my with my right hand first. After she finished making a set of prints with my right hand, she pushed my hand away. My hand brushed against my skirt, and left black ink spots on my skirt. Next, she made a set of prints with my left hand.

We walked back to the desk where Officer McGinnis was sitting. I could tell that Ms. Webber was a little nervous when she saw Officer McGinnis. Officer McGinnis did not like the idea that there was black ink on my skirt.

Ms. Webber left, I paid my bond, and I called a taxi to take me back to my job. After I entered the building, I asked the receptionist to call Ms. Smith. I spoke to Ms. Smith on the phone, and she told me I should receive a letter from her within a week. I hung up, got into my car, and drove home.

The next week I went to the police station in Grundy County and told the officer at the front desk how I was treated at my job the week before. I filed a battery report on Maria, my former coworker, and my manager, Mr. Stevens, who deliberately tried to hit my leg when we were in one of the managers' offices. I also filed a battery report on Ms. Webber for pushing my hand downward and causing my hand to brush against my skirt.

During the week, I also called a couple of attorneys because I needed someone to represent me in court. One attorney I spoke to was just as upset about the situation as I was. He told me the woman who hit me, Maria, should be put in jail. He suggested I find an attorney in the same county where I had to go to court.

The next morning I called directory assistance and asked for the names and numbers of a couple of attorneys who practice criminal law for Grundy or Livingston counties. I wrote down the names and numbers and scheduled an appointment with the first attorney I called.

When I arrived at the law office of Jason Delaney, it looked as if he and his partner were in the process of dissolving their partnership. His partner was moving out.

Mr. Delaney and I sat in the conference room. I explained what had happened at my job and that I had received a termination letter from my supervisor. Also, I told him I had already spoken to one attorney and that the attorney told me the woman who hit me on my arm should be put in jail. At the end of the conversation, Mr. Delaney told me he could take the case, but he did not practice criminal law. I really liked him and told him that surely he could handle a simple battery case. My court date was approximately two weeks away, and I was afraid I may not find another attorney in time.

Eventually, Mr. Delaney told me he would take the case. I had to pay a retainer fee, and he had to have the balance of his fee prior to going to court. I paid the retainer the same day. The following week I took the balance of the fee to his office. Mr. Delaney told me he would see me on the scheduled court date and we said good-bye.

On the first court date, Mr. Delaney asked for a continuance. To make sure my former coworker would not forget the next court date, he sent a summons to my former place of employment for the woman who hit me on my arm.

On the next court date, I went to court dressed in a dark-blue suit with a pair of high heels, and I put my hair up in a French roll. I must admit I looked like a flight attendant.

During the bench trial, the woman who hit me stuck to her story. The judge found me not guilty. My attorney and I were leaving the courtroom when Maria took a seat in the front row. I guess she wasn't finished with her charade. Mr. Delaney looked back at the judge and gave Maria a look that meant he did not like what she was doing.

That afternoon I felt completely exhausted and asked Mr. Delaney if he would like to have lunch with me. He was a little hesitant but eventually said yes. We ate at a restaurant that wasn't too far from my former job. He asked me if I wanted him to accompany me to my job for my arbitration hearing. I told him no. I thought it would be a waste of his time. I told him the people I'd worked with would probably tell him he wasn't needed anyway.

I met with Mr. Delaney at least two more times. I wanted to talk to him about a potential personal-injury case against my coworker.

It was at least six months before I received a notice about an arbitration hearing. After receiving the notice, I had to go to my former place of employment to talk to a union steward. During the six months after I was terminated, I was working at North Shore National Bank, downtown on the Magnificent Mile, an upscale section of Chicago's Michigan Avenue, running from the Chicago River to Oak Street in the Near North side.

It was a Tuesday morning, and I was sitting at my desk in the real-estate department of the bank when I received a call from my union steward. He told me he had won the arbitration case for me and asked me to choose a day when I would like to return to work. I knew that it would be in my best interest to go back to my old job.

The position I had at the bank was temporary. North Shore National Bank was in the process of merging with another bank.

Unfortunately, I could not sue my former managers or supervisors. Shortly after I was terminated from my old job, I made an appointment to speak with an attorney who practiced employment law. He told me that I would have to lose at the arbitration hearing before I could consider filing a lawsuit. He also told me that he could not file the lawsuit on a contingency basis. I did not have any money to pay for a lawsuit if I had lost my job.

Also, I did not file a lawsuit against Maria, the co-worker who hit me because my former attorney told me that it would cost approximately two thousand dollars to file a lawsuit against my former coworker.

So, the dilemma that I was in is that I had a job that was temporary and my former employer was giving me my old job back. I did not receive any back pay, but my salary was a lot more than I was making as a Secretary. The benefits were good and I had already worked at the company for ten years. I was thinking about staying there until I retired.

I was glad I had gotten my job back. I told the union steward that I would like to return to work the following week.

When I returned, I decided I would just do my job and forget about being a manager. Also, I decided to request a new work schedule. I could not tolerate being on the same shift with the people who had treated me unfairly. I changed my starting time from 8:00 a.m. to 3:00p.m.

In 1995 there was an opening for a supervisor on the job-posting board. I put in an application. Apparently, I did not pay close attention to the work schedule. The starting time was okay, but the days off were during the week, and I wanted to keep my weekends off.

Usually, the new supervisors always get weekdays off. I decided I would not apply for another supervisor position. Also, you have to fill out an application that is almost the size of a book. I felt they were requesting too much information.

Once, I applied for a sales-manager position at one of the local offices. This position is one of a few with days off on the weekend. I sent in my application and was given a date and time to report for an interview. The person who interviewed me was very nice. At the end of my interview, he told me he was going to give the position to some young guy who had just graduated from high school, but he encouraged me to apply for other positions.

The next day, I decided to file a complaint with the job-complaint office. In my complaint, I stated that I should have gotten the job because I was better qualified. In the end, the young man got the job and the job-complaint office sent me a letter stating that the young man sent in an application for the sales-manager position, and my application was for a supervisor's position. I had accidentally mailed the wrong application. To be perfectly honest, I was so fed up with the way some people are selected for higher-level positions that I really wanted to mail in a department-store application. In other words, I did not care if I sent them a job application from a local department store.

At this point in my career, I decided I'd had enough. I did not want to apply for any more supervisor or managerial positions.

I continued to work in the magazine section and the shipping department. One day, Ms. Smith asked if I would be interested in filling in for her while she took a two-week vacation. I told her I would be happy to.

I was still going to school in the evenings. It wasn't long before I graduated with a bachelor's degree in business administration. After graduation, I started working on my master's degree, but rather than finish my master's, I decided I wanted to go to law school.

I am an alumni at the university I graduated from, but I felt as though I wanted to be part of another organization. I looked in the telephone directory for some nonprofit organizations. I found one I wanted to be part of. The women's voting rights group.

I attended a meeting in Lansing, Illinois, where I met a couple of people who told me a lot about the organization. I found out that they had a number of local chapters in the suburbs, and their main office is located in downtown Chicago. The women's voting rights group also has chapters in other countries.

One of the members and I became good friends. Ms. Peterson is a little older than I am, but she worked diligently to attract new members to our chapter in Lansing.

She wanted me to become president of the Lansing chapter at some point, but I told her I wanted to be part of a larger group and become more involved in different activities. Ms. Peterson expressed to me that she had wanted to become a state legislator, but for some reason or another, she didn't pursue the idea when she was younger. A state legislator position is a good position to have because they are the people who make the laws that govern the citizens in our state. I got the feeling she was wondering what my thoughts were about the job. Again, it was not a job that I would have considered at that time because I really wanted to work with people in the public sector.

With the help of this woman, I got involved in registering people to vote in the state of Illinois. After I received my deputy registrar's card, instructions, and registration cards for new voters, she and I, on behalf of the women's voting rights group, would set up a table at different locations and encourage people to fill out the voter's registration cards to become a registered voter if they weren't already.

Eventually, I contacted the main office in downtown Chicago. I went to one of the monthly meetings and decided I wanted to be part of this group. At the meeting, I was given a sheet of paper with several grass-roots issues to choose from (for example, mercury, death penalty, criminal justice, immigration, gun violence, etc.).

You picked an issue you wanted to work on, and at the monthly meetings, you reported on your issue.

My interest was in criminal justice. There were at least one or two people at the meeting who worked on the same issue, and everyone usually worked with one or two other organizations that were working on these issues.

For example, one of the members and I worked on criminal-justice Issues. Both of us were included in meetings with other organizations that worked with ex-offenders and people with a criminal record. The woman I worked with had been working with the women's rights group for a number of years. She specialized in issues concerning juveniles in the criminal-justice system. She also attended meetings with different organizations that were involved in helping juvenile offenders.

My main interest was in the adult male and female prison populations, ex-offenders, and the criminal courts. During the time that I worked with this organization, I was hoping I could bring some people (faith-based organizations, school administrators, citizens in the community) together to start a reentry program for ex-offenders that involved skill training and education. I thought it would be good to have a skill-training center accessible to people in Markham and Harvey, Illinois. I also feel that a skill-training center was needed in Chicago Heights and Ford Heights, Illinois. If these centers are established, they will not only benefit ex-offenders but could provide skill training and education to people who cannot afford to pay for the training or education that they would receive at the centers.

During one of the meetings I attended at the women's voting rights group office in downtown Chicago, one of the members suggested it would be nice to have a commission here in Illinois that monitors judicial conduct.

A few years ago, I contacted a law firm here in Chicago regarding a commission on judicial conduct. I got the impression that the attorneys were interested in establishing this commission. I am not in contact with the women's voting rights group or the law firm at this time. I have not heard any more about a commission on judicial conduct. I think it would be beneficial for the people in the state of Illinois, and I hope they and other states will pursue this idea.

When I worked with this nonprofit organization, I felt the time I spent going to different meetings and speaking to people here in Illinois and other states helped to make a difference in people's lives. There is still a lot of work to be done on all the Issues that concern the people in this state and all over the country, but I believe the nonprofit group I worked with is a great organization. I wish more people could become actively involved in working with the criminal-justice system and other grass-root issues that affect us all.

At work, I would share a lot of the information I had learned about the criminal-justice system with my coworkers. My supervisor knew I was attending these different meetings and working on criminal-justice issues. I did not take a lot of time off from work. When I needed a day off, my request was usually granted.

Several people at my job had formed a van pool. After I found out how much cheaper it was to ride the van, I signed up. A few months later I took the road test to become a back-up driver. I passed and received my driver's certificate.

On days I had to go downtown, I would take the Metra Train there and back. Once I arrived at the train station, I would get into my car, go home, eat lunch, and drive to the place where I would get on the van and ride forty miles to work. I followed this routine for a number of years until I got tired of all the commuting and decided to schedule a day off whenever I had to attend a meeting.

Riding the van to and from work is a lot cheaper than driving. The only bad part is when the van-pool members would have disagreements, and one or two of them would fabricate a story just to get someone put out of the van. This was mostly done to create a hardship for someone. There were a couple of people who seemed to enjoy creating problems for other people. The problem I encountered with some of them was a little different than what some of the other members encountered.

It was a Saturday afternoon around one thirty. I and several other people were sitting in our cars in the parking lot, waiting for the van to arrive. Ordinarily I do not work on Saturdays, but I had signed up to request overtime. As I stated earlier, I am also a back-up driver, and today I was supposed to drive the van to work.

I was reading a pamphlet when Danielle McGhee, a coworker, pulled into the parking space behind me and hit my back bumper at the same time I raised my head. The impact made my head jerk backward. I got out of my car to assess the damage to my car. My neck was hurting, and I told her I was going to call the police so I could make out an accident report.

In the meantime, the van arrived to take us to work. Danielle did not want to wait for the police. Since I was driving the van that day, I insisted we wait until the police arrived.

The police officer arrived shortly. I explained how the accident happened and told him I had a neck injury. The officer made out the report and gave me a copy. Afterward, I got into the van and drove us to work.

The next day I made an appointment to see my doctor and found an attorney who would represent me in my personal-injury case. I contacted the insurance company listed on the report to report the accident, and I told the claim representative that I hired an attorney to represent me in my claim against the insurance company.

A couple of days after the accident, I went downtown to the law office of John Kessler to meet with him regarding my personal-injury case. I figured I might get exactly what my claim was worth. A few years ago, someone told me that if I ever needed an attorney for a personal-injury case, I should try to find one in downtown Chicago. I knew the attorneys with offices downtown probably paid a lot for the rental space, so I figured he would work diligently to resolve my case. In other words, the rent is expensive, so I'm sure that the attorneys want to get as much as they possibly can in order to keep paying the rent and all of the other bills that they have. I gave Mr. Kessler a copy of my accident report, and he gave a contract to sign. The contract stated he would be taking my case on a contingency basis, and he would get 33.3 percent of any money received from the insurance company, but if he had to file a lawsuit, his fee would be 40 percent of any money I receive.

Mr. Kessler instructed me to start physical-therapy treatments as soon as possible and to contact him once I finished. I thanked him for taking my case and went home.

During the same week, I went to see my doctor. I told him about the accident and I that my neck was hurting. After examining me, he told me I had whiplash, and he gave me a referral form to take to physical therapy.

I went to PT twice a week for the next three months. My physical therapist massaged my neck and shoulders and gave me barbells to lift. At the end of my physical-therapy treatments, my neck was not completely healed, but I was ready to stop the treatments.

After my last PT treatment, I called Mr. Kessler and told him I was finished. He told me he would be sending a letter to the insurance company with my medical bills, lost wages, etc., so he could make a request for compensation for my injuries, pain, and suffering.

Approximately one month after I had spoken to my attorney, Ms. Taylor, a claims representative from the insurance company, called and asked me if I would like to set up a meeting at one of their offices, or at my attorney's office. I told her I would like to meet with her downtown at my attorney's office.

When I arrived at Mr. Kessler's office, Ms. Taylor was already there. The three of us went into the conference room for our meeting. After we all sat down, Ms. Taylor told me she would not be able to pay anything on my claim. I asked her what was wrong. She said she received a statement from one person who was sitting in the parking lot at the time of the accident, and that person had stated I backed into the vehicle that was in back of my car. Remember—my car was in park, and I was sitting there reading a pamphlet.

Next, she showed me a letter from another person I work with, but this person was not a member of our van pool, and she was on vacation at the time of the accident. My attorney did not make any statements, he simply looked at me.

The two individuals who made the false statements are friends with the woman who hit my car.

Mr. Kessler told me the woman who hit my vehicle was claiming she hit my car intentionally, therefore I cannot collect any money from the accident. I asked Mr. Kessler if that was the end of my claim, and he said nothing else could be done. I told him he should file a lawsuit because the people who stated they were witnesses to the accident had fabricated their stories, and I did not believe Danielle, the woman who was driving the Jeep, hit my car intentionally.

It is possible that the insurance representative thought that Danielle hit my car out of spite or envy. My first thought was that the insurance representative assumed that Danielle hit my car so that I could file a claim against the insurance company. Perhaps Danielle tried to file a claim against my insurance company. I was the injured party in this accident and I am not the one who was at fault. Danielle is not a friend of mine, so there is no way that the insurance representative could have thought that Danielle was trying to do me a favor.

I believe that the insurance company should have paid my claim. Since they refused to pay the claim, I still believe that my attorney should have filed a lawsuit.

One day when I was at work, I was thinking about the personal-injury case again. I was wondering why I did not think to file a complaint with the attorney's complaint and administration division.

The contract I signed with my attorney stated that if he had to sue, his fee would be 40 percent of whatever money I received from the insurance company. Well, I was injured in the accident, and the insurance company did not want to pay anything for my injuries, pain, and suffering. Now, I am beginning to wonder why Mr. Kessler did not want to file a lawsuit.

Certainly I could have gone to the police and told them a woman claimed she hit my car intentionally. I simply cannot believe an attorney does not want to go to court when someone intentionally hits your car and you're injured and you do not receive any money from the insurance company. I should have contacted another attorney, but I just figured that that was the end of it and there was nothing else that I could do.

I feel that I was treated unfairly by the insurance company and my attorney. Let's be real: you know Danielle was not telling the truth when she asked one of her friends to type a letter for the insurance company. Danielle's friend stated she was at the scene of the accident, but in actuality, she was nowhere near the scene. How easy it would have been to reveal that the woman who wrote the letter was not at the parking lot at the time, and she wasn't even a member of our van pool.

Well, I guess I should thank God that I had a job and a paycheck every two weeks.

I just want to mention that I have filed a lawsuit in civil court in the past. Ordinarily, I would not pro se a lawsuit. This lawsuit involved another individual who I had a disagreement with. A couple of attorneys had already told me I didn't have a lawsuit, but I wanted to go to court anyway.

At the time, I did not consider my lawsuit to be frivolous, but I was hoping that the judge may have thought of something that the attorneys I consulted with hadn't thought of. I knew the judge was going to dismiss my case, but I was really surprised by what I saw when I went to court. There were people lined up along the wall. I assumed they were attorneys. After I sat down, I noticed there was not an empty seat in the courtroom, but that was not the only thing I noticed: I was the only black person in the courtroom.

Now, the only thing I could think was that something was not right with this picture. There were attorneys lined up against the wall, but for some reason or another I did not feel they were suing on behalf of black people. If they were, I wondered why I did not see any black people in the courtroom. Next, I said to myself that I was sure most people live the same type of existence, so why do these white people have lawsuits and black people were not represented here? Lastly, I could only assume but was pretty sure cases were being heard in this courtroom five days a week. To be perfectly honest with you, I believe that these courtrooms have looked the same way for the past 50 years. I do not believe that black people have received the same type of representation in civil court as white people.

When my case was called, I walked up to the judge's bench, and as I have already stated, I knew I did not have a case. The judge was very nice to me. He said I did not have a case and asked if I wanted to amend my complaint. I told him no and thanked him for taking the time to read my complaint and for giving me his opinion.

After I left, I felt satisfied. I did not have a lawsuit, but I was glad I took the time to go downtown and file my complaint. Being the only black person in this civil court made me realize something is not right with our civil-court system. Some reforms are definitely needed within our civil- and criminal-court system.

The next day I returned to work, and I continued working in the magazine section and spending my free time working on criminal-justice Issues.

As I mentioned earlier, I really did not want to apply for anymore supervisor or management positions. I was passionate about working as a criminal justice issue specialist for the women's voting rights group.

Chapter 4

New Changes
at My Place of Employment

Some changes were taking place at my job. We had two or three different managers within the past ten years, and I noticed there were approximately ten to fifteen new employees. I believe the new employees were all related. I know Jagirdar Gupta, a woman who worked with me, had three sons and a daughter who worked at the magazine distribution center along with five or six of their cousins.

A couple of Jagirdar's cousins wanted to become supervisors. Jodhaa started working as a supervisor in the shipping department approximately one year after she began working for the company. I did not have a lot of problems with her, but I could not understand why she would deliberately bump me whenever she walked behind me. Also, these people had a bad habit using the n-word. I really dislike it when someone calls me a n-----. Jagirdar frequently made the following statement to me:

"People used to put a whip on your backs." The word "your" was referring to black people.

At the time, we had a new logistics manager, Ms. Lauren Caldwell, in the shipping department. One day I overheard Ms. Caldwell tell Jagirdar that she wished she could do something to cause me to lose my job.

I really don't know why Ms. Caldwell dislikes me.

If you will recall, Maria is the co-worker who hit me on my arm several years ago. When I returned to work, Maria was working in a temporary supervisor's position. One day she walked past me and she waived a sheet of paper in my face as she said "Hi".

I immediately went to the nearest telephone and called the police. It was around three thirty. After the police arrived, the secretary paged Maria for several minutes, but she did not answer her page.

Everyone assumed that she had left for the day, so the police left without her.

I was still angry about what she did when I was training to be manager. I refused to let her taunt me. That is why I called the police.

Ms. Caldwell likes Maria and I believe that is why she wants me to lose my job.

Naturally, Jagirdar would do anything whatsoever if she thought she could win some favors from the manager.

To make a long story short, Jagirdar fabricated a story about me. She said I had shouted some profanities at her in the hallway. Jodhaa and Rishi, two of her nieces, corroborated her story. I did not curse Jagirdar, nor have I ever cursed any other individual at my place of employment.

My supervisor, Ms. Smith, called me into her office to ask what had happened in the ladies bathroom. I told her I was simply walking past Jagirdar when she stopped me and asked me, "What's your problem?" I told her I told Jagirdar I do not have a problem and I continued to walk to my locker.

Ms. Smith told me the manager from the shipping department would be in to talk to me. She asked me to sit in the conference room. Approximately fifteen minutes passed before Ms. Caldwell walked into the conference room and handed me a termination letter. I did not sign it and told her I wanted to give the letter to my union steward before I left the building.

It took about two weeks for the union steward to win my case. He contacted me at home and said I had to sign a "last-chance agreement letter" before I could return to work. I explained that I did not do anything wrong and felt it was ridiculous for me to sign this agreement. In the end, I signed it and went back to work. The time off from work was considered a long-term suspension, so I did not receive any back pay for the time I was off.

After a few years, the managers stopped issuing last-chance agreement letters, and my letter was removed from my employee folder.

There were other times when I was harassed by different people, but I did not let it bother me. Ms. Caldwell was nice when she wanted to be. One day she asked if I wanted to be a supervisor again. I told her I wasn't interested. Ms. Caldwell was friendly with Maria, the woman who hit me on my arm in the ladies locker room in 1993.

In 2005, three of my coworkers and I were riding in the van when the driver made a left turn about two blocks from my place of employment. A woman who was driving a red car in the lane next to us also made a left turn. After she turned left, she veered into our lane and struck the left side of our van. The van jumped the curb, and I was literally thrown out of my seat. My leg hit the hard plastic arm rest on the seat in front of the bench seat in the back of the van. I did not know my leg was injured until I stood to see what was happening. When I stood up, I hollered in pain.

You are probably telling yourself that you already know how this story is going to end.

Well, after the police were called and an officer made out an accident report, we went to work. The next day I noticed that my leg was bruised. I called my doctor's office to schedule an appointment. I looked in the telephone directory for an attorney so I could file a claim against the insurance company. This time I decided to find an attorney whose office was a lot closer to home.

I made an appointment with Nathan Jones. When I went to his office, he told me the insurance companies were not paying him the amount of money they should have been paying. He told me if the insurance company did not want to pay what he felt the claim was worth, he would file a lawsuit.

Approximately three weeks later, I went to see my doctor. I found out I had nerve damage in my right leg. After my doctor's visit, I scheduled an appointment with a chiropractor. Then I started physical-therapy treatments as soon as possible.

A couple of months had passed, and I was going to the chiropractor twice a week for my physical-therapy treatments. During my physical-therapy treatments, I was given leg massages and heat therapy for my leg. I would leave home around three in order to be at work by four o'clock. One day while I was working on the computer, when Mark, a coworker, walked past me and said, "We're going to stop the lawsuit." I was surprised by his statement. I thought, *Some people are just mean and jealous.*

I just wanted to concentrate on my physical therapy and do the job I was being paid to do. I was also anxiously waiting for the day when my leg would feel better and I could stop my physical-therapy treatments. I knew that once my treatment ended, my attorney would send a demand letter to the insurance company requesting compensation for my injuries, pain, and suffering. I also knew he would file a lawsuit if the insurance company did not offer to pay us a reasonable amount of money.

In the meantime, some of my coworkers had heard about the accident and just assumed my attorney was going to file a lawsuit once they heard that he had sent a private investigator to take a statement from two of the people who were riding in the van with me at the time of the accident.

I don't know why there was so much hostility from a couple of my co-workers. I don't know how these people found out about my lawsuit. I certainly did not tell them that my attorney was considering filing a lawsuit.

They probably figured out that I was going to file a lawsuit because I was walking with a slight limp. I knew that my injury was permanent and I assume that it was obvious to everyone else.

Michelle, the woman who was driving the van is one of the individuals who gave a false statement to the insurance company when Danielle, her girlfriend, hit my car in 2001.

It was her cousin, Mark, who came to me and said, "We're going to stop the lawsuit". I don't know why he thought that he and his cousin were going to stop my lawsuit, or why they thought they were in a position to stop my lawsuit.

Approximately one year later I contacted my attorney and told him I had finished physical therapy. Mr. Jones told me he had requested a copy of the officer's police report. When I spoke to Mr. Jones, he told me that the woman who was driving the car stated that her husband was driving. Also, she stated the driver of our van struck her vehicle.

I did not get the opportunity to read the police report, but I think it is pretty sad that the officer wanted to believe her instead of the four of us in the van. There is no way the driver of our van hit her vehicle. She stated that after the van hit her vehicle, he turned to the right and jumped the curb. Really, that is not logical.

At the end of physical therapy, Mr. Jones submitted my medical bills, lost wages, etc. to the insurance company. He asked for a reasonable amount of money for my claim. The insurance company sent him a letter with an offer that was less than reasonable. The amount they offered us would not pay for groceries for three months. Now don't forget, my attorney would get one-third of the money I received, and the chiropractor had to be paid.

Mr. Jones told me that he was going to file a lawsuit. I told him that I wanted a copy of the lawsuit. He was very hesitant about giving me a copy of the lawsuit. Finally, I told him that I will stop by his office to pick up a copy of the lawsuit.

I was not very happy when I received a copy of the lawsuit. He put Christina Marrero as the defendant. The insurance company was not named in the lawsuit. I called Mr. Jones and I asked him why he did not include the insurance company in the lawsuit. Of course, I knew that he could add the insurance company at a later date. Mr. Jones told me that he could not sue the insurance company once they have made us an offer. This totally contradicts what he told me when I signed the contract in his office. Mr. Jones told me that he would sue if the insurance company did not offer us a reasonable amount of money.

Mr. Jones filed a lawsuit in the county where the accident occurred. Unfortunately, the other ladies in the van became jealous when they heard my attorney had filed a lawsuit. (They had to be notified because they had to appear in court as witnesses.)

Mr. Jones told me I did not have to appear in court on the first date or any subsequent court dates unless we have a jury trial. It took about six months for Mr. Jones to locate Ms. Marrero, the woman who had hit our van. Apparently, she had moved several times since the accident.

When Mr. Jones went to court, the two ladies who were witnesses had to appear in court too. I was not there.

For the next couple of months, I called Mr. Jones's office and did not get an answer. I went to his office to find out if anyone was there. I went upstairs and looked through the glass in the front door.

Everything was just as it was the first day I met with him in his office. I tried calling his cell phone number, but he stopped answering.

Eventually, I decided to ask Dana, one of the ladies who was on the van, what happened when they went to court. She told me that the judge looked at her and Michelle and said, if you want to kill, no bond. She also told me that one of the attorneys in the court room was telling my attorney, it's only ten thousand dollars, whatever that means.

Later that day, another coworker walked past me and said, "Your attorney may be related to me."

This does not seem to be important, except for the fact that this particular coworker is a friend of all the people who made false accusations the last time I was involved in a car accident.

The next morning I called the clerk's office at the courthouse. She informed me that my attorney had filed a motion for a leave to re-file, and the judge had dismissed the case for lack of due diligence.

I could not believe what I had just heard. Mr. Jones did not call me to tell me what was happening with my lawsuit. I still have a permanent injury to my leg and I had a lawsuit, but my attorney did not do his due diligence, nor did he re-file the lawsuit. In other words, my attorney did not show up in court when he was scheduled to be there. I did not get one cent for my injury, pain, and suffering.

After I found out that the judge had dismissed my case, I contacted the Judicial Investigation Bureau to file a complaint against the judge. I felt that he should have separated the two issues: the no bond issue and my lawsuit.

The letter that I received from the judicial investigation bureau did not indicate that they have found any wrong doing by the judge.

This lawsuit was just another example of how you can hire an attorney for a personal-injury case and not get any money.

I was very upset because I have a permanent injury to my right leg. If Mr. Jones had told me that he could no longer work on my case, I would have looked for another attorney who could.

I eventually reported Mr. Jones to the attorneys' complaint and administration division.

I found out he'd become sick while working on my lawsuit and was not able to continue. Also, I was told that the attorney's decisions concerning how to pursue the matter involved matters of legal opinion and strategy, with respect to which lawyers have broad discretion.

My interpretation of the above sentence is simply stated. My attorney chose to stop going to court after the judge made his statement to the two witnesses that were in court.

My disagreements with Mr. Jones's strategy and legal opinions did not provide the attorneys' complaint and administration division with a basis for bringing formal disciplinary charges. I should have filed a legal-malpractice lawsuit, but I did not have any money.

Without any monetary compensation, I feel I have not received any justice or satisfaction. So far I have had two personal-injury cases and have not received one cent from either.

If you thought this last case was bad, just wait until you read this last story.

*

Everything was going okay at my place of employment. My lawsuit was dismissed in 2009. After that, I needed some time to myself. I took a couple of days off from work. I had planned to take a short vacation after I received the money from the lawsuit. Unfortunately, I did not get a chance to have a jury trial and ended up with nothing.

There is one good thing that I can say about Ms. Caldwell: she allowed most of the employees to sign up for overtime. The extra money really helped a lot. I was a single mother with a lot of bills to pay. I did not expect my son to help me pay for bills that I had made. There were times he did not have a job. When I worked overtime, I could work two extra hours a day and one weekend day. For two or three years I would put my name on the overtime schedule and would always sign up to work holidays. Even though I made a decent salary, it did not seem to be enough money. After I started working overtime, there were times when my yearly income increased somewhat. There were times when I got tired of working overtime, but as I stated earlier, it make life better for me.

In March 2011, I had a bad cold and was on sick leave for three days. I had previously signed up to work on the weekend following my days off. It was a Friday when I called Ms. Caldwell's secretary to find out if I was scheduled to work. I was feeling a little better and needed the money. The secretary told me I was scheduled to work. Ms. Caldwell was not in the office at the time. The secretary told me she was sure that it would be okay for me to work on Saturday.

Usually, if you are scheduled to work on a weekend or holiday, you must report to work. If you do not show up, you may receive some disciplinary action.

I felt a little reluctant about going to work Saturday, even though I knew I would be returning home if Ms. Caldwell had not given me permission to work that day. When I arrived, I put my things in my locker and went straight to the manager's office. Ms. Caldwell was not in. I went out to the workroom floor to look for a supervisor.

Ms. Johnson was supervising. When I located her, I explained to her that I had called Ms. Caldwell the day before to find out if she wanted me to work. Ms. Johnson said she would put my name on her time sheet and that I should go ahead and start working in the magazine section.

She assigned another woman, Tonya Thompson, to work with me. Tonya and I had to sort the bundles of magazines and place labels on them before putting them onto the trucks. The conversation between Tonya and I was strictly job-related. At the time, Tonya was dating Luis. I have had some problems with Luis in the past.

Sometimes I would stop at the seven eleven store after work to buy something to snack on while I was driving home. A few of my coworkers would stop there after work.

Luis was arrested at the local seven eleven store a few years ago because he was trying to get the sales clerk to find a couple of guys who would attack me at the store. This happened during the time that I was waiting for my lawsuit to be filed.

Well, getting back to my story about Tonya, his girlfriend.

I asked Tonya if she wanted me to place the shipping labels on the bundles and send them down the conveyor belt to her so she could load them into the carts. She told me it would be okay with her. Next, I went to look for the equipment that we needed in order to facilitate the distribution of the magazines. I helped her set everything up and started printing the labels. Within two or three hours, we had labeled and distributed all the magazines in our area.

I was waiting for the tractor driver to bring us some more magazines. Tonya was standing next to the conveyor belt and had her cell phone in her hands. I waited for about fifteen minutes before I decided to page Ms. Johnson on the intercom system. When she called me back, I told her there weren't any more magazines for us to label and distribute. Ms. Johnson told me she would check to see if there were more on the workroom floor. Also, I asked her if she could move me to another area in the shipping department. I told her I wanted to work with someone else.

I really didn't have any issues with Tonya, but I could tell that she really did not care for me. I will never forget the time when Luis came to our work area to speak to her once and he was holding her around her waist. Her back was facing me and he was hugging her and looking at me and I heard him say the word n-----. Instantly, I knew that he was calling me the n-word.

I did not report the incident to my supervisor because I knew that he was still angry about being arrested and having to go to court. Of course, it was his fault. Anything that happened to him in court, he brought on himself. I have never said or done anything to make these people dislike me.

Ms. Johnson moved me to a different section. About two hours later, Ms. Caldwell's secretary was paging me. When I walked into Ms. Caldwell's office, she asked me to sit in the conference room. A few minutes later, she walked in, sat down, and told me Tonya said I "cursed her, called her ugly, and told her she was the worst person I have ever worked with."

As you have probably guessed, I was very surprised, even shocked by what I was hearing from my manager. I never said any of those things to Tonya or anyone else.

Next, Ms. Caldwell asked me for my ID badge and told me I should go to the locker room and take everything out of my locker. I am sure that Ms. Caldwell didn't believe Tonya's story, but Ms. Caldwell liked Luis, Tonya's boyfriend, and she probably wanted to do something to satisfy him.

Shortly after Luis had been arrested, he came to work and when he saw me in the hallway, he looked at me and he made the statement: I am not going to stop until you are as angry as I am. I really don't know what he meant by this statement.

Let's not forget, Ms. Caldwell is also friendly with Maria.

I asked Ms. Caldwell if there was a union steward on duty. I told her I wanted to explain the situation to the union steward, and hopefully we could resolve the matter. She told me it didn't matter, that she had to give me a termination letter.

Before I left the building, I stopped in the union room to see if a union steward was available. No one was in the union room, but I did see Luis in the hallway. He told me he didn't have anything to do with the situation. I left the building and went home.

The following week, I called the union office. The union steward I wanted to speak to was not available, so I left my name and number for him to call me back. Later that evening I received a call from Alex, the steward. I told him exactly what had happened, about the false allegations Tonya made against me. He told me he would get a copy of the termination letter and would call me back.

The next day I called the police station in Grundy County where the incident took place and told them about the false allegations my coworker made against me. I wanted them to have some sort of documentation regarding the incident. I probably should have gotten into my car and driven the forty miles to the station. I called the police station to make a report, but I am not sure it the police documents everything when you call the station.

At the end of the week, Alex called me again to tell me he had a copy of my termination letter and that since the union had a backlog of cases, it may take a year or two before my case went to arbitration.

The next morning I called Anthony, the president of the union, and he told me the same thing. After I hung up, I sat down and thought about the situation. I decided to call the state attorney's office in Livingston County. I told him about the false allegations against me and that I had contacted the police department, but I did not ask the police officer if he had made a written report. I just knew no one would believe Tonya's story when it came time for the arbitration hearing.

I asked the state's attorney if he could file criminal charges against Tonya. He told me I had to speak to the state's attorney in the county where the incident took place. Again, I thought it would not be necessary in order to win my arbitration case. After all, Tonya's story was ludicrous. So I decided not to get into my car and drive forty miles to the courthouse in Grundy County.

The following week I contacted the unemployment office and applied for benefits. It took a while for me to complete the process. At some point I had to participate in a conference call with my former supervisor and a law judge. After a four-to-six-week waiting period, I finally received unemployment benefits.

While I was unemployed, I sent out some job applications on the computer and went to different companies to fill out applications. I recall getting a telephone call from a retail store to come in for a group interview.

During the Interview, I found out the position was temporary. I really was not interested in a temporary position but applied anyway. I noticed that all the interviewees were anywhere from fifteen to twenty years younger than I was. I did not get the job. I filled out approximately fifty to one hundred applications during my job search.

While I was unemployed, I stayed in contact with my union steward. In March 2012, I received a call from Alex, and he told me my arbitration case was scheduled for April 2012. He informed me that he and Laura Mackey, vice president of the union, would meet with me to discuss the case. He told me we could meet somewhere close to where I lived. I suggested we meet at the village hall.

A couple of days after our phone conversation, I met with the union representatives at the village hall. I told them what had happened the day I was terminated and also told them about some problems I'd had in the past with some of my coworkers. I told them why I felt Tonya made the false allegations against me.

I told my union representatives that I believe that Tonya made the false allegations against me so that I could be fired. She probably thought that my termination would make her boyfriend happy.

As I mentioned earlier, I don't know why her boyfriend feels as if he has to do something to me. It's almost as if he feels that he has to prove a point.

Our meeting lasted approximately one hour. Prior to the end of our meeting, Alex told me he should not have a problem winning my case. Laura told me she wanted us to have the next meeting at the magazine distribution center.

The following week, I met with Alex and Laura at my former place of employment. We entered the building through the main entrance. The secretary led us into one of the conference rooms. Once we were seated, Laura asked me to tell them exactly what happened on the day I was terminated. Then they asked me to repeat my story. They asked me the same questions over and over again. After telling them what happened, Alex told me Tonya said she texted one of her friends and told her what was happening while we were waiting for the tractor driver to bring some more magazines to our area.

Next, Alex told me it was possible to retrieve a copy of the text message. I told him I thought it would be a great idea to get a copy. I said, "Alex, if Tonya did text someone, and she told this person all the things she alleged I have said or done, then she had this well planned in advance, and someone was helping her." I told him there was no way someone could consider her story credible.

Laura told me that during the arbitration hearing, she and the arbitrator (an attorney) will be asking me some questions, and I should only answer yes or no. I could say things such as "Yes I did" or "No I did not." She also stated that she and the arbitrator will be questioning Tonya, my former supervisor, and some more people from the job. The last thing she told me was, "You can usually tell if a person is telling the truth whether the person looks you in the eye when he or she is speaking to you."

I told her I always look a person in the eye when I am speaking to him or her.

Next, she told me she wanted me to look directly at her when I am answering any questions. She also told me she would take her index finger and tap on her nose so I would remember to look in her eyes.

At that point we ended our meeting, and the vice president of the union made a statement. She told me she has never lost a case in front of this arbitrator. She gave me a pat on the shoulder and we said good-bye.

Chapter 5

Arbitration Hearing

In April 2012, the arbitration hearing was held at JDT's Magazine Distribution Center. Upon arriving at my former place of employment, I parked in front of the building and went in through the main entrance. I walked past one of the smaller offices and saw Tonya, my supervisor, and the shipping manager.

During the arbitration hearing, the following people were present: the arbitrator, the union steward, a secretary, a representative from Human Resources, and the union vice president, Laura. I was sitting next to Laura.

The secretary had made a copy of my personnel folder for everyone. The representative from Human Resources had a stack of documents (cases that some people had filed in court).

First, the arbitrator looked at us and said, "We have repeat offenders."

I am assuming that the arbitrator meant that I was fired once before, and she was probably insinuating that I had done something wrong.

If you will recall, Maria attacked me the first time that I was terminated. This time, I have done absolutely nothing wrong.

Next, she told us that she arbitrates in several different states. Before starting the hearing, she told us she would be recording it and then proceeded to turn on her tape recorder. A couple of people walked into the conference room and gave their testimony. My former supervisor gave her testimony, but it had nothing to do with the day in question. She wanted to talk about some interactions that I had with some former coworkers. Apparently, she went to these people and asked them to write a statement about our working relationship. Ms. Caldwell was there to testify. One other lady gave her testimony. I don't recall what she said, because it had nothing to do with the day that I was terminated. I believe she worked in employee relations.

The arbitrator and the union steward asked them about my character.

When Tonya walked in and sat down to give her testimony, she began talking and crying. She even asked for a box of Kleenex. I was not allowed to interrupt or make any comments during the hearing. I had one comment I wanted to make and wrote it down on the notepad in front of me and slid it over to Laura, the vice president of the union.

When it was time for me to answer questions from the arbitrator or the union vice president, I could only answer yes I did or no I did not. Previously, Laura told me that if I said anything other than yes or no, it could open the door for a number of other issues and it would take a lot more time to discuss them. During the hearing, I became a little disgusted with the whole process. The other people who testified were not at work on the day in question. Tonya got the opportunity to make her false allegations. I did not get to tell the story about what happened that day.

During my last meeting with Laura, she told me it was my word against Tonya's. Given the fact that there were no witnesses, I should win my case.

At the end of the hearing, I heard Laura tell the arbitrator that the business agent who represented me in my arbitration case in 1993 had retired, but she had spoken to him recently. She stated that he told her she should let me keep my job.

The arbitrator told us we should get her answer in approximately four weeks. Afterward, the representative from Human Resources told the arbitrator she had more cases that she may want to read and dropped them in front of her.

After the arbitration hearing ended, Laura and I were talking in the hallway. She told me she thought everything should be fine. She gave me a hug and said good-bye.

I was really hoping everything worked out in my favor. After all, I did not do any of those things Tonya had accused me of doing. Also, I wanted my job back so I could work for another ten or twelve years and possibly get a managerial position and an increase in salary. Most of all, I wanted the money that I was supposed to receive in back pay. The amount should have been equal to one year's salary.

Approximately four weeks after the arbitration hearing, I contacted Laura to find out if she'd heard anything from the arbitrator.

She told me the arbitrator did not give me my job back and that she had a copy the arbitrator's decision and would mail it to me. I received a copy of the decision within two business days. In her decision, she upheld the false allegations that Tonya had made.

In the meantime, the unemployment office was also waiting for a copy of the arbitrator's decision (award letter). I typed a statement, giving my account of what happened on the day I was terminated, and I attached it to the copy of the arbitrator's award letter. I took everything to the unemployment office.

A short time after the hearing, I decided to file a complaint with the attorneys' complaint and administration division. I was very upset about losing the arbitration case. In my complaint, I stated that the arbitrator made the same false allegations that Tonya made, and I felt she and Tonya should receive criminal charges.

In other words, I feel that the arbitrator is going along with the person who made the false allegations against me. She may have recorded all of the information and had her secretary to type it up, but in her award letter, she states that I said the things that Tonya accused me saying. It sounds like she is making the same false allegations. She knows that there was no reason for her to decide against me. It was my word against Tonya's. There were no witnesses, so I should have gotten my job back.

I do not recall the exact wording of the letter addressing the final disposition of my complaint, but essentially, it stated they did not find any evidence that indicate that the attorney's complaint and administration division should proceed with any type of disciplinary action.

I spoke to one attorney before contacting the attorneys' complaint and administration division, and he told me it is not the same if an arbitrator records the information, has her secretary type it up, and present it to someone in an award letter.

What matters is that I did not do anything wrong, my former coworker made false allegations against me, and the arbitrator decided against me at my hearing.

Now, I have no job and no money simply because Tonya made false allegations against me and the arbitrator agreed with Tonya in her award letter.

This is 2015, but sometimes I feel as though it is 1915. I feel I have been treated unfairly. Whenever I had a case involving money, I did not receive any. I feel as though there are a lot of people in this city and throughout the country who do not want honest people to have good-paying jobs or money in their bank accounts. It seems dishonesty often has an unfair advantage. I guess they were more convincing at lying than I was at telling the truth.

I would like to see technical schools, junior colleges, universities, and skill-training centers that will help poor people learn a skill or get a college education. At the present time, there are some universities that offer a free education for poor, underprivileged people, particularly through scholarships and financial aid. I'm sure that there are a lot of people who want a college degree.

There was a time in my life when I felt sad because I did not have a college degree, but I continued to pursue my education until I received my degree.

Education is important, and I hope all people get a chance to become better educated.

About the Author

Growing up in Chicago is about D. A. Slone's personal experiences, some frustrating, dealing with Chicago's legal system, as well as the time she spent working with various nonprofit organizations. She has a bachelor's degree in business administration.

She lives in a suburb of Chicago. This is her first book.

Printed in the United States
By Bookmasters